MEDITERRANEAN DIET COOKBOOK FOR SENIORS 2025

Delicious and Nutritious Recipes for a Vibrant, Active Life

DR. HARRY C. EDGAR

All rights reserved. @ 2024 by Dr. Harry C. Edgar No part of this book may be reproduced, distributed, or transmitted in any form or by any means, including photocopying, recording, or other electronic or mechanical methods, without the prior written permission of the publisher, except in the case of brief incorporated quotations. in critical reviews and certain other non-commercial uses permitted by copyright law.

CONTENTS

20-DAY MEAL PLAN 7

INTODUCTION 2

Overview of the Mediterranean Diet: History, Benefits, and Core Principles 4

How the Mediterranean Diet Supports Healthy Aging 5

Essential Nutrients for Seniors: Vital Vitamins, Minerals, and Antioxidants 6

Kitchen Essentials: Tools, Ingredients, and Pantry Staples 8

Tips for Making Cooking Easier and More Enjoyable as You Age 9

1 10

ENERGIZING BREAKFASTS FOR A BRIGHT START 10

2 18

HEART-HEALTHY LUNCHES FOR VITALITY 18

3 24

SATISFYING DINNERS FOR BALANCED NUTRITION 24

4 34

WHOLESOME SNACKS AND LIGHT BITES 34

5

NOURISHING DESSERTS AND SWEET TREATS 42
SHOPPING LIST 50
CONCLUSION 52

Dear Reader

I want to extend my deepest thanks to all the wonderful readers who picked up this book! Writing Mediterranean diet cookbook for seniors 2025

It has been a journey filled with passion, dedication, and a genuine desire to help others live healthier, more vibrant lives.

Your decision to adopt this guide means a lot to me. Whether you are just beginning your journey to better health or have been on this path for some time, I hope that the recipes and tips contained in these pages serve as a valuable and practical resource.

If you found this book helpful and inspiring, I would greatly appreciate it if you would take a moment to share your honest thoughts in a review. Your comments not only help others discover this book but also motivate me to continue sharing useful ideas for a healthier life.

Thank you for being part of this journey and for a future full of vitality and well-being!

20-DAY MEAL PLAN

Day 1	
Breakfast: Greek Yogurt Parfait with Fresh Berries and Honey	
Lunch: Quinoa Salad with Cucumber, Feta, and Mint	
Dinner: Baked Salmon with Lemon and Dill	
Day 2	
Breakfast: Mediterranean Veggie Omelet with Feta and Herbs	
Lunch: Lentil and Vegetable Soup with Fresh Herbs	
Dinner: Chicken Souvlaki with Tzatziki Sauce	
Day 3	
Breakfast: Oatmeal with Nuts, Seeds, and Fruit Compote	
Lunch: Tuna Salad with Olive Oil and Chickpeas	
Dinner: Stuffed Bell Peppers with Ground Turkey and Brown Rice	
Day 4	
Breakfast: Avocado Toast with Tomato and Olive Oil	
Lunch: Greek Salad with Kalamata Olives and Lemon Vinaigrette	
Dinner: Shrimp and Zucchini Noodles with Garlic and Olive Oil	
Day 5	
Breakfast: Spinach and Feta Breakfast Wraps	
Lunch: Roasted Vegetable and Hummus Wrap	
Dinner: Ratatouille with Fresh Herbs and Garlic	
Day 6	
Breakfast: Greek Yogurt Parfait with Fresh Berries and Honey	
Lunch: Quinoa Salad with Cucumber, Feta, and Mint	
Dinner: Baked Salmon with Lemon and Dill	
Day 7	
Breakfast: Mediterranean Veggie Omelet with Feta and Herbs	
Lunch: Lentil and Vegetable Soup with Fresh Herbs	
Dinner: Chicken Souvlaki with Tzatziki Sauce	
Day 8	
Breakfast: Oatmeal with Nuts, Seeds, and Fruit Compote	
Lunch: Tuna Salad with Olive Oil and Chickpeas	
Dinner: Stuffed Bell Peppers with Ground Turkey and Brown Rice	
Day 9	
Breakfast: Avocado Toast with Tomato and Olive Oil	
Lunch: Greek Salad with Kalamata Olives and Lemon Vinaigrette	
Dinner: Shrimp and Zucchini Noodles with Garlic and Olive Oil	
Day 10	
Breakfast: Spinach and Feta Breakfast Wraps	
Lunch: Roasted Vegetable and Hummus Wrap	
Dinner: Ratatouille with Fresh Herbs and Garlic	
Day 11	
Breakfast: Greek Yogurt Parfait with Fresh Berries and Honey	
Lunch: Quinoa Salad with Cucumber, Feta, and Mint	
Dinner: Baked Salmon with Lemon and Dill	
Day 12	

Breakfast: Mediterranean Veggie Omelet with Feta and Herbs	Day 17
Lunch: Lentil and Vegetable Soup with Fresh Herbs	Breakfast: Mediterranean Veggie Omelet with Feta and Herbs
Dinner: Chicken Souvlaki with Tzatziki Sauce	Lunch: Quinoa Salad with Cucumber, Feta, and Mint
Day 13	Dinner: Chicken Souvlaki with Tzatziki Sauce
Breakfast: Oatmeal with Nuts, Seeds, and Fruit Compote	Day 18
Lunch: Tuna Salad with Olive Oil and Chickpeas	
Dinner: Stuffed Bell Peppers with Ground Turkey and Brown Rice	Breakfast: Avocado Toast with Tomato and Olive Oil
Day 14	Lunch: Tuna Salad with Olive Oil and Chickpeas
Breakfast: Avocado Toast with Tomato and Olive Oil	Dinner: Stuffed Bell Peppers with Ground Turkey and Brown Rice
Lunch: Greek Salad with Kalamata Olives and Lemon Vinaigrette	Day 19
Dinner: Shrimp and Zucchini Noodles with Garlic and Olive Oil	Breakfast: Greek Yogurt Parfait with Fresh Berries and Honey
Day 15	Lunch: Greek Salad with Kalamata Olives and Lemon Vinaigrette
Breakfast: Greek Yogurt Parfait with Fresh Berries and Honey	Dinner: Shrimp and Zucchini Noodles with Garlic and Olive Oil
Lunch: Roasted Vegetable and Hummus Wrap	Day 20
Dinner: Baked Salmon with Lemon and Dill	Breakfast: Oatmeal with Nuts, Seeds, and Fruit Compote
Day 16	Lunch: Roasted Vegetable and Hummus Wrap
Breakfast: Spinach and Feta Breakfast Wraps	Dinner: Ratatouille with Fresh Herbs and Garlic
Lunch: Lentil and Vegetable Soup with Fresh Herbs	
Dinner: Ratatouille with Fresh Herbs and Garlic	

INTRODUCTION

Welcome to Mediterranean Diet Cookbook for Seniors 2025, a compilation inspired by the foods, tastes, and lifestyle that have kept me healthy. I vividly recall the day I decided to try the Mediterranean diet. I had been feeling sluggish, with pains that appeared to sneak into my joints and drain my vitality. It was harming not just my physical well-being, but also my view on life. After hearing so much about the Mediterranean diet, I started studying, and what I found was incredible.

Adopting this diet was more than simply tasting new foods; it was about adopting a way of life that values whole, fresh ingredients, heart-healthy oils, and vivid, nutrient-dense meals. I observed a difference from week to week. My energy began to improve, those tenacious pains began to fade, and my stomach, which had become a frequent source of anxiety, began to relax. This was not a limiting diet or a passing fad; it was a long-term lifestyle that fed both my body and spirit.

One of the most pleasant discoveries was how delicious the meals were. I wasn't giving up flavor to feel better; just the contrary! Fresh tomatoes, olives, robust grains, and the unique taste of fruits made every meal feel like a small celebration. And, although other diets may focus exclusively on nutrition, the Mediterranean approach values balance, sharing, and joy in the kitchen, making each meal something to look forward to.

This cookbook is my way of sharing these advantages with you. It's developed with seniors in mind, with meals that are simple but tasty, easy to digest, and high in nutrients that benefit aging bodies. From invigorating breakfasts to gratifying dinners, you'll find dishes that are not only tasty but also designed to promote a lively, healthy lifestyle. If you want to feel more energized, reduce inflammation, and embrace a really delightful way of eating, you've come to the correct spot. Let's take this Mediterranean vacation together and cherish every minute!

LET GET STARTED!!

Overview of the Mediterranean Diet: History, Benefits, and Core Principles

The Mediterranean diet is more than simply a meal plan; it is a cultural inheritance of food traditions that originated in Mediterranean Sea-bordering areas such as Greece, Italy, and southern Spain. The diet originated thousands of years ago as a way of life in which societies relied on fresh, seasonal, and locally sourced ingredients. The Mediterranean method was publicly acknowledged in the mid-twentieth century, when researchers discovered exceptionally low rates of heart disease and other chronic diseases in these cultures despite limited access to modern treatment. This finding resulted in the Mediterranean diet being a symbol of long-term health and energy.

At its heart, the Mediterranean diet emphasizes fruits, vegetables, whole grains, legumes, and nuts, with olive oil serving as the main fat source. Fish, poultry, and dairy are consumed in moderation, but red meat and processed foods are limited. Herbs and spices are key, adding flavor without relying on too much salt. Meals are typically shared, which fosters a strong sense of community and attention when eating.

The advantages of the Mediterranean diet have been extensively researched. According to studies, it can considerably lower the risk of heart disease, stroke, and type 2 diabetes, in part because it emphasizes healthy fats, antioxidants, and fiber. Its anti-inflammatory properties make it an excellent nutritional choice for promoting joint health, cognitive function, and even mood stability. This diet is neither restricted or temporary; rather, it is a long-term lifestyle that naturally promotes a healthy weight and balanced blood sugar levels.

This diet encourages a slower, more thoughtful manner of eating, appreciating nutritious foods that energize the body and heal the spirit. The goal is to appreciate the colors, textures, and tastes of each component rather than calculating calories. Finally, the Mediterranean diet offers a plan for good aging, blending traditional wisdom with cutting-edge nutritional research to provide an engaging path toward wellbeing. Whether you want to enhance your health or simply adopt a more balanced, pleasant approach to eating, the Mediterranean diet provides timeless counsel.

How the Mediterranean Diet Supports Healthy Aging

The Mediterranean diet has become a health beacon, particularly for the elderly, due to its role in boosting lifespan, vigor, and quality of life. This diet, based on the typical eating habits of Mediterranean Sea-bordering nations, emphasizes fresh vegetables, fruits, whole grains, lean meats, and heart-healthy fats like olive oil. Together, these substances provide a variety of nutrients that can considerably promote healthy aging, assisting seniors in maintaining mental clarity, joint health, and even emotional well-being.

One of the most notable advantages of the Mediterranean diet is its influence on cardiovascular health. This diet, which is high in antioxidants from fruits and vegetables and omega-3 fatty acids from fish, promotes heart health by decreasing inflammation and lowering blood pressure. Such anti-inflammatory benefits are critical for older persons, as chronic inflammation has been related to illnesses such as arthritis, hypertension, and even cognitive impairment.

In terms of cognitive health, research demonstrate that the Mediterranean diet can play an important role in maintaining brain function. Leafy greens, berries, nuts, and fatty fish have all been linked to improved cognition and a lower risk of neurodegenerative illnesses. This is especially crucial for seniors, as memory and cognitive sharpness might fade with age.

Beyond physical health, the Mediterranean diet promotes emotional well-being. This diet contains nutrients such as B vitamins, magnesium, and omega-3s, which can help regulate mood, reduce stress, and potentially relieve depression symptoms. This can be life-changing for seniors who want to live not just a longer, but also a happier life.

The Mediterranean diet is a way of life, not simply food. It promotes social relationships, unhurried meals, and a balanced approach to eating that values enjoyment over restriction. This comprehensive approach is ideal for seniors, promoting mindful eating habits that can lead to healthier, more sustainable lifestyles. Adopting the Mediterranean diet allows older folks to enjoy not just a more vibrant, active lifestyle, but also the invaluable gift of time spent in good health and spirits.

Essential Nutrients for Seniors: Vital Vitamins, Minerals, and Antioxidants

As we age, our nutritional needs shift, demanding a unique focus on specific vitamins, minerals, and antioxidants essential for healthy aging. For seniors, maintaining vitality isn't just about what we eat but choosing nutrients that best support our bodies' changing requirements. With the right nutrition, it's possible to manage energy, protect cognitive health, boost immune resilience, and support bone strength well into our golden years.

1. Vitamin B12

Vitamin B12 is essential for brain health, red blood cell production, and maintaining energy. As we age, our ability to absorb B12 from food decreases, making it crucial to incorporate B12-rich foods like fish, eggs, and fortified cereals or consider a supplement if levels are low.

2. Vitamin D

Vitamin D aids calcium absorption, which is key to bone health and preventing osteoporosis. For seniors, sun exposure alone may not provide enough vitamin D, so it's beneficial to add foods like salmon, fortified milk, or even a supplement to support bone density and immune function.

3. Calcium

Calcium partners with vitamin D to keep bones strong and healthy. For seniors, inadequate calcium intake increases the risk of bone fractures. Dairy products, leafy greens, and fortified alternatives like almond milk are excellent sources to help preserve bone health.

4. Magnesium

Magnesium supports muscle function, heart health, and immune response. It's also known for reducing blood pressure. Since magnesium intake often decreases with age, foods like nuts, seeds, and whole grains are vital to meet daily requirements.

5. Omega-3 Fatty Acids

Omega-3s found in fish, flaxseeds, and walnuts are beneficial for heart and brain health. These healthy fats reduce inflammation, support cognitive function, and even improve mood.

6. Antioxidants

Antioxidants like vitamins C and E combat oxidative stress, a major factor in aging. By reducing cell damage, antioxidants support immune function and skin health. Brightly colored fruits and vegetables like berries, citrus fruits, and leafy greens provide a spectrum of antioxidants crucial for seniors.

By including these essential nutrients, seniors can nurture their bodies, protect their minds, and truly thrive in their later years, ensuring that they remain active, vibrant, and resilient as they age.

Kitchen Essentials: Tools, Ingredients, and Pantry Staples

- When embracing the Mediterranean diet, it's essential to stock your kitchen with the right tools, ingredients, and pantry staples that bring this healthy, flavorful eating style to life. Whether you're preparing a traditional Mediterranean feast or a quick weeknight meal, the essentials in your kitchen can make all the difference.
- Tools: For efficient Mediterranean cooking, you don't need an extensive collection of gadgets. A sharp chef's knife is essential for chopping fresh herbs, vegetables, and meats. A large, heavy-bottomed skillet or sauté pan will help you make flavorful Mediterranean stews or quickly sauté vegetables and seafood. A quality mortar and pestle can be invaluable for grinding spices like cumin and coriander, releasing their full flavor. Investing in a good olive oil dispenser ensures you're always ready to add a drizzle of the region's liquid gold to your dishes.
- Ingredients: At the heart of the Mediterranean diet are fresh, wholesome ingredients. Stock your kitchen with fresh fruits and vegetables such as tomatoes, cucumbers, eggplants, and peppers—these are staples for Mediterranean salads, stews, and sides. Whole grains like bulgur, quinoa, and couscous make great bases for a variety of meals, offering fiber and nutrients. Beans and legumes like chickpeas, lentils, and fava beans are protein-packed and versatile, perfect for soups or salads. Olive oil is the cornerstone of Mediterranean cooking, offering healthy fats and antioxidants.
- Pantry Staples: To enhance your cooking, your pantry should include a range of Mediterranean spices and condiments. Oregano, thyme, cumin, and sumac are just a few of the spices that add depth and complexity to Mediterranean dishes. Tahini, balsamic vinegar, and Dijon mustard are essential for making dressings and sauces. Stock canned goods like tomatoes, artichokes, and olives to add flavor and convenience to your meals.
- A well-stocked Mediterranean kitchen isn't just about having the right ingredients—it's about setting the stage for healthy, delicious meals that nourish the body and mind

Tips for Making Cooking Easier and More Enjoyable as You Age

- As you age, cooking can become a bit more challenging, but with a few practical tips, it can remain a fun, enjoyable, and manageable activity. Here's how you can make cooking easier and more rewarding as you grow older:
- Invest in Ergonomic Tools: As joint pain and mobility concerns increase, kitchen gadgets designed to reduce strain are a game changer. Tools like ergonomic knives, angled peelers, and jar openers can make food prep significantly easier. Consider investing in a non-slip cutting board to help stabilize ingredients and reduce the risk of injury
- Simplify Your Setup with Appliances: Slow cookers, air fryers, and Instant Pots are perfect for seniors. These "set it and forget it" devices allow you to prepare meals with minimal supervision, freeing you up to relax or do other tasks. Appliances that reduce standing time and stirring can be lifesavers
- Stock Up on Staples: Keeping your pantry, fridge, and freezer well-stocked with essentials ensures that cooking becomes less of a hassle. Canned beans, rice, pasta, and frozen vegetables can be lifesavers when you need a quick meal. Additionally, pre-chopped vegetables and pre-cooked grains help you save valuable time
- Batch Cooking and Leftovers: Batch cooking meals in large portions and storing leftovers can make your life so much easier. Cooking in bulk and freezing meals for later reduces the stress of daily meal prep. Plus, repurposing leftovers into new dishes keeps things fresh and interesting
- Create a Comfortable Cooking Environment: Don't forget about your kitchen environment. Ensuring your space is well-lit and clutter-free can help improve focus and safety. Additionally, using music or an audiobook can make cooking feel more like a pleasurable activity than a chore

ENERGIZING BREAKFASTS FOR A BRIGHT START

Greek Yogurt Parfait with Fresh Berries and Honey

Preparation Time: 10 minutes

Cooking Time: None

Serving Size: 1 serving

Ingredients:

- 1 cup plain Greek yogurt
- ½ cup mixed fresh berries (blueberries, strawberries, raspberries)
- 1 tablespoon honey
- 2 tablespoons granola or chopped nuts (optional)

Procedure:

- Start by spooning half of the Greek yogurt into a glass or bowl.
- Layer half of the fresh berries on top of the yogurt.
- Drizzle half of the honey over the berries.
- Repeat the layers with the remaining yogurt, berries, and honey.
- Sprinkle granola or chopped nuts on top if desired for added crunch.

Nutritional Values (per serving):

- Calories: 200 kcal
- Protein: 15g
- Carbohydrates: 25g
- Fiber: 4g
- Sugars: 18g
- Fat: 5g

- **Health Benefits**: Greek yogurt is high in protein and probiotics, promoting gut health and muscle maintenance. Fresh berries provide antioxidants and vitamin C, supporting immune health and reducing inflammation. Honey adds natural sweetness and may have antimicrobial properties, while granola or nuts contribute healthy fats and fiber.

Mediterranean Veggie Omelet with Feta and Herbs

Preparation Time: 10 minutes

Cooking Time: 10 minutes

Serving Size: 1 omelet

Ingredients:

- 2 large eggs
- ¼ cup chopped spinach
- ¼ cup diced tomatoes
- 2 tablespoons diced onions
- 2 tablespoons crumbled feta cheese
- 1 tablespoon fresh herbs (parsley, dill, or basil)
- Salt and pepper to taste
- 1 teaspoon olive oil

Procedure:

- In a bowl, whisk the eggs with salt and pepper.
- Heat olive oil in a skillet over medium heat. Sauté the onions for 1-2 minutes until soft.
- Add the tomatoes and spinach, cooking until wilted, about 2-3 minutes.
- Pour the eggs over the vegetables in the skillet. Let the eggs cook for 2 minutes, then sprinkle feta cheese and fresh herbs on top.
- Fold the omelet in half and cook for another 1-2 minutes until eggs are fully set.
- Serve hot with additional herbs if desired.

Nutritional Values (per serving):

- Calories: 180 kcal
- Protein: 12g
- Carbohydrates: 5g
- Fiber: 1g

- Sugars: 2g
- Fat: 13g
- Health Benefits: Eggs are a great source of protein, essential amino acids, and choline, supporting brain and muscle health. Feta cheese offers calcium and probiotics, while tomatoes and spinach add fiber, vitamins A, C, and K. Fresh herbs enhance flavor and are rich in antioxidants.

Oatmeal with Nuts, Seeds, and Fruit Compote

Preparation Time: 5 minutes

Cooking Time: 10 minutes

Serving Size: 1 bowl

Ingredients:

- ½ cup rolled oats
- 1 cup water or milk of choice
- 1 tablespoon mixed nuts (almonds, walnuts)
- 1 tablespoon mixed seeds (chia, flax, pumpkin)
- ¼ cup fresh or dried fruit compote (blueberries, raspberries)
- Honey or maple syrup to taste (optional)

Procedure:

- In a small saucepan, bring water or milk to a boil. Add the oats and reduce the heat to low, simmering for 5-7 minutes, stirring occasionally until thickened.
- While the oats cook, prepare the fruit compote by gently heating fresh or dried fruit in a small pan until soft and juicy.
- Once the oats are done, transfer them to a bowl. Top with nuts, seeds, and a spoonful of fruit compote.
- Add a drizzle of honey or maple syrup for sweetness if desired.

Nutritional Values (per serving):

- Calories: 250 kcal
- Protein: 8g
- Carbohydrates: 35g
- Fiber: 6g
- Sugars: 12g

- Fat: 8g

Health Benefits: Oats are high in soluble fiber, which aids digestion and helps manage cholesterol. Nuts and seeds provide healthy fats, fiber, and protein, promoting satiety and heart health. The fruit compote offers antioxidants and vitamins, supporting immunity and skin health.

Avocado Toast with Tomato and Olive Oil

Preparation Time: 5 minutes

Cooking Time: None

Serving Size: 1 slice

Ingredients:

- 1 slice whole-grain bread
- ½ ripe avocado, mashed
- 2-3 cherry tomatoes, sliced
- 1 teaspoon extra-virgin olive oil
- Salt and pepper to taste
- Fresh basil or parsley for garnish (optional)

Procedure:

- Toast the slice of whole-grain bread to your desired crispness.
- Spread the mashed avocado evenly over the toast.
- Arrange the tomato slices on top of the avocado.
- Drizzle with olive oil and season with salt and pepper.
- Garnish with fresh basil or parsley if desired.

Nutritional Values (per serving):

- Calories: 220 kcal
- Protein: 4g
- Carbohydrates: 18g
- Fiber: 6g
- Sugars: 2g
- Fat: 16g

Health Benefits: Avocado is rich in monounsaturated fats, supporting heart health and skin vitality. Tomatoes provide antioxidants, particularly lycopene, which can reduce the risk of certain cancers. Olive oil adds healthy fats, and whole-grain bread contributes fiber for digestive health.

Spinach and Feta Breakfast Wraps

Preparation Time: 10 minutes

Cooking Time: 5 minutes

Serving Size: 1 wrap

Ingredients:

- 1 whole-wheat tortilla
- 1 cup fresh spinach
- 2 tablespoons crumbled feta cheese
- 1 large egg, scrambled
- Salt and pepper to taste
- 1 teaspoon olive oil

Procedure:

- In a skillet, heat olive oil over medium heat. Add the spinach and cook until wilted, about 1 minute.
- Push the spinach to the side and pour in the beaten egg, cooking until scrambled, about 2 minutes.
- Season with salt and pepper, then remove from heat.
- Place the scrambled egg and spinach mixture in the center of the tortilla. Sprinkle with feta cheese.
- Fold the tortilla over the filling, creating a wrap. Serve immediately.

Nutritional Values (per serving):

- Calories: 250 kcal
- Protein: 10g
- Carbohydrates: 20g
- Fiber: 5g
- Sugars: 1g
- Fat: 15g

Health Benefits: Spinach provides iron, vitamin K, and antioxidants, supporting energy and bone health. Feta adds protein and calcium, while eggs contribute high-quality protein. Whole-wheat tortillas add fiber, promoting fullness and supporting digestive health.

HEART-HEALTHY LUNCHES FOR VITALITY

Quinoa Salad with Cucumber, Feta, and Mint

Preparation Time: 15 minutes

Cooking Time: 15 minutes

Servings: 4

Ingredients:

- 1 cup quinoa, rinsed
- 2 cups water
- 1 cucumber, diced
- 1 cup cherry tomatoes, halved
- ½ cup feta cheese, crumbled
- ¼ cup fresh mint leaves, chopped
- ¼ cup fresh parsley, chopped
- 3 tbsp extra-virgin olive oil
- 1 lemon, juiced
- Salt and pepper to taste

Procedure:

- In a medium pot, bring water to a boil, add quinoa, and reduce to a simmer. Cook for 15 minutes, until the quinoa is frothy.. Allow to cool.
- In a large bowl, combine the quinoa, cucumber, cherry tomatoes, feta, mint, and parsley.
- In a small bowl, whisk together olive oil, lemon juice, salt, and pepper.
- Drizzle dressing over the salad and toss gently to combine.

Nutritional Values (per serving):

- Calories: 260
- Protein: 7g
- Carbohydrates: 23g
- Fiber: 4g
- Fat: 12g

Health Benefits:

- This quinoa salad is rich in fiber, healthy fats, and plant-based protein. Quinoa provides essential amino acids, while olive oil and fresh herbs promote heart health and aid in reducing inflammation.

Lentil and Vegetable Soup with Fresh Herbs

Preparation Time: 15 minutes

Cooking Time: 35 minutes

Servings: 6

Ingredients:

- 1 cup green or brown lentils, rinsed
- 1 tbsp olive oil
- 1 onion, diced
- 2 carrots, diced
- 2 celery stalks, diced
- 2 cloves garlic, minced
- 1 zucchini, diced
- 1 can (14 oz) diced tomatoes
- 4 cups vegetable broth
- 1 tsp cumin
- ½ tsp thyme
- Salt and pepper to taste
- ¼ cup fresh parsley, chopped

Procedure:

- In a large pot, heat olive oil over medium heat. Sauté onion, carrots, and celery until softened.
- Add garlic, cumin, and thyme, stirring for 1-2 minutes.
- Add lentils, zucchini, tomatoes, and broth. Bring to a boil, then decrease the heat and simmer for 30 minutes or until the lentils are cooked..
- Season with salt and pepper. Stir in parsley just before serving.

Nutritional Values (per serving):

- Calories: 180
- Protein: 9g
- Carbohydrates: 30g
- Fiber: 8g
- Fat: 4g

Health Benefits:

- This soup is packed with fiber, protein, and essential nutrients. Lentils are a great source of plant-based protein, while the vegetables provide antioxidants and vitamins to support immune health and digestion.

Tuna Salad with Olive Oil and Chickpeas

Preparation Time: 10 minutes

Cooking Time: None

Servings: 4

Ingredients:

- 1 can (14 oz) chickpeas, drained and rinsed
- 1 can (5 oz) tuna in olive oil, drained
- ½ cup cherry tomatoes, halved
- ½ cucumber, diced
- 2 tbsp red onion, finely chopped
- ¼ cup fresh parsley, chopped
- 3 tbsp extra-virgin olive oil
- Juice of 1 lemon
- Salt and pepper to taste

Procedure:

- In a large bowl, combine chickpeas, tuna, cherry tomatoes, cucumber, red onion, and parsley.
- In a small bowl, whisk together olive oil, lemon juice, salt, and pepper.
- Drizzle the dressing over the salad and toss gently to combine.
- **Nutritional Values (per serving):**
- Calories: 320
- Protein: 18g
- Carbohydrates: 22g
- Fiber: 6g
- Fat: 16g

Health Benefits:

- This salad provides a balance of protein and fiber, supporting heart health, muscle maintenance, and digestion. Tuna and olive oil offer anti-inflammatory omega-3 fatty acids, while chickpeas add fiber and complex carbohydrates.

Greek Salad with Kalamata Olives and Lemon Vinaigrette

Preparation Time: 10 minutes

Cooking Time: None

Servings: 4

Ingredients:

- 2 cups Romaine lettuce, chopped
- 1 cup cherry tomatoes, halved
- 1 cucumber, sliced
- ½ red onion, thinly sliced
- ½ cup Kalamata olives
- ½ cup feta cheese, crumbled
- ¼ cup extra-virgin olive oil
- Juice of 1 lemon
- 1 tsp dried oregano
- Salt and pepper to taste

Procedure:

- In a large bowl, combine lettuce, tomatoes, cucumber, red onion, olives, and feta.
- In a small bowl, whisk together olive oil, lemon juice, oregano, salt, and pepper.
- Drizzle the dressing over the salad and toss gently to coat.

Nutritional Values (per serving):

- Calories: 220
- Protein: 5g
- Carbohydrates: 8g
- Fiber: 3g
- Fat: 18g

Health Benefits:

- This Greek salad is rich in healthy fats, fiber, and antioxidants. Kalamata olives and olive oil contribute to heart health, while vegetables and feta offer a range of vitamins and minerals that support skin, bone, and immune health.

Roasted Vegetable and Hummus Wrap

Preparation Time: 15 minutes

Cooking Time: 20 minutes

Servings: 4

Ingredients:

- 1 zucchini, sliced
- 1 red bell pepper, sliced
- 1 cup mushrooms, sliced
- 1 red onion, sliced
- 2 tbsp olive oil
- Salt and pepper to taste
- 4 large whole-grain tortillas
- 1 cup hummus
- 1 cup fresh spinach leaves

Procedure:

- Preheat the oven to 400°F (200°C). Arrange zucchini, bell pepper, mushrooms, and onion on a baking sheet. Drizzle with olive oil, season with salt and pepper, and roast for 20 minutes, until the veggies are soft.
- Spread a layer of hummus on each tortilla, then add a handful of spinach and a portion of roasted vegetables.
- Roll up each wrap, slice in half, and serve.

Nutritional Values (per serving):

- Calories: 300
- Protein: 8g
- Carbohydrates: 40g
- Fiber: 8g
- Fat: 12g

Health Benefits:

- This wrap provides a balanced blend of fiber, protein, and antioxidants. Roasted vegetables offer vitamins A and C, supporting skin health and immunity, while hummus adds plant-based protein and fiber for satiety and digestion support.

SATISFYING DINNERS FOR BALANCED NUTRITION

Quinoa Baked Salmon with Lemon and Dill

Preparation Time: 10 minutes

Cooking Time: 20 minutes

Servings: 4

Ingredients

- 1 cup quinoa, rinsed
- 1 1/2 cups water
- 4 salmon fillets (4-6 oz each)
- 1 lemon, sliced thinly
- 2 tbsp olive oil
- Salt and pepper to taste
- Fresh dill, chopped (about 1/4 cup)
- 1 tbsp garlic powder
- 1/2 tsp paprika (optional)

Procedure

- Preheat the oven to 375°F (190°C) and line a baking sheet with parchment paper.
- In a medium saucepan, bring water to a boil and add quinoa. Reduce to a simmer, cover, and cook for approximately 15 minutes, or until quinoa is soft and water has been absorbed.. Fluff with a fork.
- Prepare the salmon: Place salmon fillets on the prepared baking sheet. Brush each with olive oil and season with salt, pepper, and garlic powder.
- Arrange lemon slices on top of each fillet and sprinkle fresh dill over the top.
- Bake salmon for 15-20 minutes, or until it flakes easily with a fork.
- Serve each salmon fillet over a bed of cooked quinoa, garnished with fresh herbs if desired.

Nutritional Values (per serving)

- Calories: 380
- Protein: 28g
- Carbohydrates: 30g
- Fat: 18g
- Fiber: 5g

Health Benefits

- Salmon provides omega-3 fatty acids, essential for heart and brain health. Quinoa is high in fiber, supporting digestion, and rich in minerals like magnesium and iron. The dish is an excellent source of antioxidants and anti-inflammatory properties, thanks to dill and lemon.

Chicken Souvlaki with Tzatziki Sauce

Preparation Time: 15 minutes (plus 1 hour for marination)

Cooking Time: 15 minutes

Servings: 4

Ingredients

- For Chicken Souvlaki:
- 1 lb boneless, skinless chicken breast, cut into cubes
- 2 tbsp olive oil
- 2 tbsp lemon juice
- 1 tbsp dried oregano
- 1 clove garlic, minced
- Salt and pepper to taste
- For Tzatziki Sauce:
- 1 cup Greek yogurt
- 1/2 cucumber, grated and drained
- 1 clove garlic, minced
- 1 tbsp lemon juice
- 1 tbsp fresh dill, chopped
- Salt and pepper to taste

Procedure

- Marinate the chicken: In a bowl, combine olive oil, lemon juice, oregano, garlic, salt, and pepper. Add the chicken cubes, cover, and marinate for at least 1 hour.
- Prepare Tzatziki Sauce: Mix yogurt, cucumber, garlic, lemon juice, and dill in a bowl. Season with salt and pepper to taste. Chill until ready to serve.
- Cook the chicken: Preheat a grill or skillet over medium heat. Thread the marinated chicken onto skewers and cook for 10-15 minutes, turning occasionally until fully cooked.

- Serve chicken with a generous side of Tzatziki sauce.

Nutritional Values (per serving)

- Calories: 290
- Protein: 32g
- Carbohydrates: 5g
- Fat: 15g
- Fiber: 1g

Health Benefits

- Chicken Souvlaki is high in protein, making it excellent for muscle health. The Tzatziki sauce, made from Greek yogurt, provides probiotics for gut health. The combination of herbs like oregano and dill boosts immunity and adds anti-inflammatory benefits.

Stuffed Bell Peppers with Ground Turkey and Brown Rice

Preparation Time: 15 minutes

Cooking Time: 30 minutes

Servings: 4

Ingredients

- 4 large bell peppers, tops cut off and seeds removed
- 1 lb ground turkey
- 1 cup cooked brown rice
- 1 small onion, diced
- 2 cloves garlic, minced
- 1 can diced tomatoes (14 oz)
- 1 tbsp olive oil
- 1 tsp dried oregano
- Salt and pepper to taste
- Fresh parsley for garnish

Procedure

- Preheat the oven to 375°F (190°C) and line a baking dish with parchment.
- In a skillet, heat olive oil over medium heat. Sauté onions and garlic until softened.
- Add ground turkey and cook until browned. Stir in cooked rice, diced tomatoes, oregano, salt, and pepper.
- Spoon the mixture into each bell pepper and place them in the baking dish. Cover with foil.
- Bake for 30 minutes, then remove foil and bake for an additional 10 minutes. Garnish with fresh parsley before serving.

Nutritional Values (per serving)

- Calories: 350
- Protein: 27g
- Carbohydrates: 32g
- Fat: 12g

- Fiber: 8g

Health Benefits

- Bell peppers are high in vitamins C and A, which are essential for immune health. Ground turkey is lean and protein-packed, and brown rice offers complex carbohydrates for steady energy.

Shrimp and Zucchini Noodles with Garlic and Olive Oil

Preparation Time: 10 minutes

Cooking Time: 10 minutes

Servings: 4

Ingredients

- 1 lb shrimp, peeled and deveined
- 4 medium zucchinis, spiralized into noodles
- 3 tbsp olive oil
- 3 cloves garlic, minced
- Salt and pepper to taste
- Fresh parsley, chopped

Procedure

- In a skillet, heat 2 tbsp olive oil over medium heat. Add garlic and sauté until fragrant.
- Add shrimp and cook until pink, about 4-5 minutes. Season with salt and pepper.
- Remove shrimp from skillet and add remaining olive oil. Sauté the zucchini noodles for 2-3 minutes, or until soft.
- Combine shrimp with zucchini noodles, sprinkle with fresh parsley, and serve.

Nutritional Values (per serving)

- Calories: 230
- Protein: 22g
- Carbohydrates: 8g
- Fat: 15g
- Fiber: 3g

Health Benefits

- Zucchini noodles are low in calories and high in fiber, aiding digestion. Shrimp provides lean protein and is a good source of iodine, which supports thyroid health.

Roasted Ratatouille with Fresh Herbs and Garlic

Preparation Time: 15 minutes

Cooking Time: 45 minutes

Servings: 4

Ingredients

- 1 large eggplant, diced
- 2 zucchinis, diced
- 1 bell pepper, diced
- 1 onion, diced
- 3 cloves garlic, minced
- 2 tbsp olive oil
- 1 tsp fresh thyme, chopped
- Salt and pepper to taste
- Fresh basil for garnish

Procedure

- Preheat the oven to 400°F (200°C) and line a baking sheet with parchment.
- Toss all vegetables with olive oil, thyme, garlic, salt, and pepper. Spread evenly on the baking sheet.
- Roast for 45 minutes, stirring halfway through.
- Garnish with fresh basil and serve.

Nutritional Values (per serving)

- Calories: 180
- Protein: 4g
- Carbohydrates: 25g
- Fat: 9g
- Fiber: 7g

Health Benefits

- Ratatouille is rich in antioxidants from a variety of vegetables, promoting cellular health. Eggplant and bell pepper support heart health, and the dish is naturally anti-inflammatory, ideal for seniors looking to support overall health.

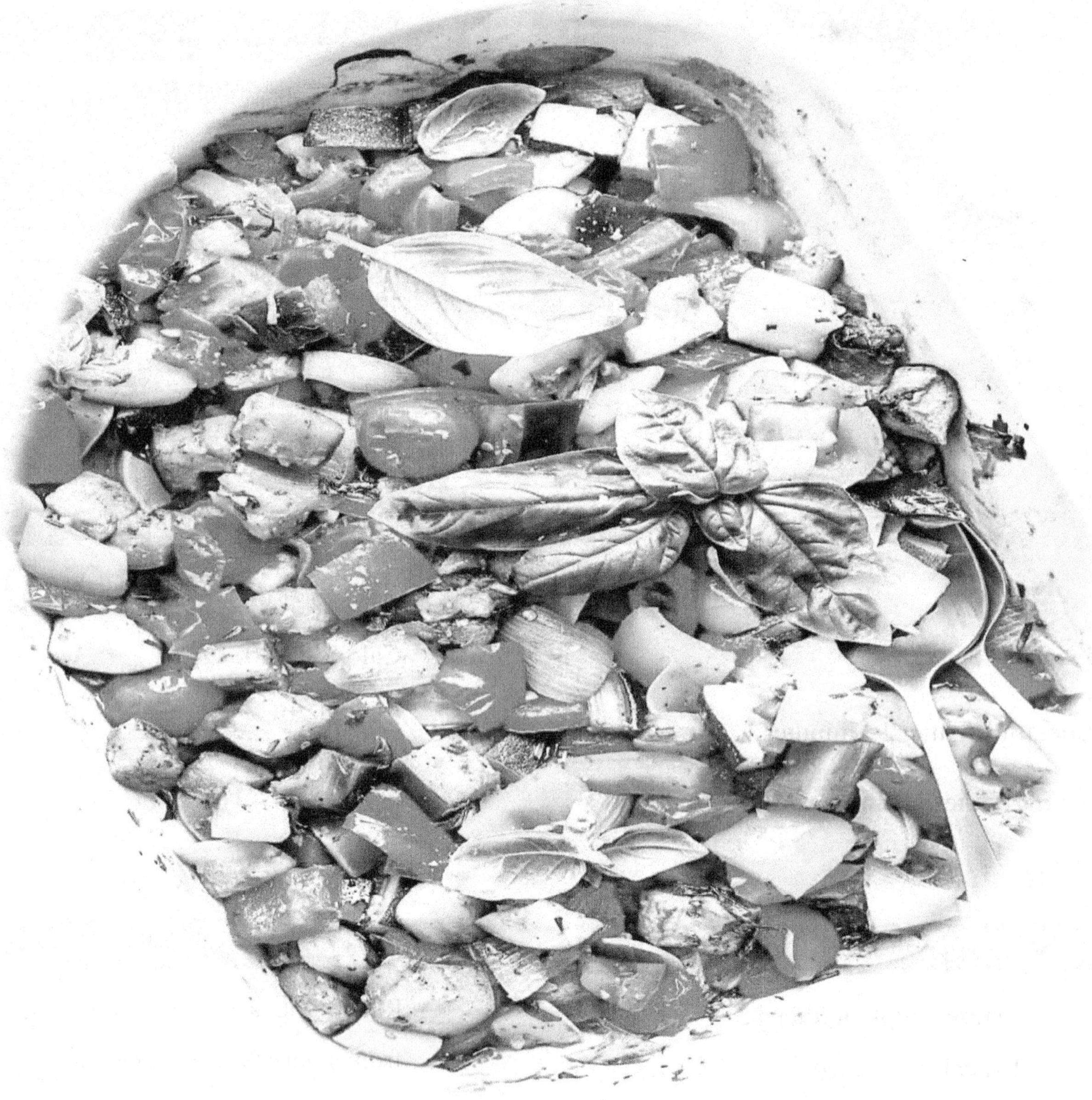

4

WHOLESOME SNACKS AND LIGHT BITES

Stuffed Grape Leaves with Rice and Herbs

Preparation Time: 45 minutes

Cooking Time: 40 minutes

Servings: 6-8

Ingredients

- 1 jar (16 oz) grape leaves in brine, rinsed and drained
- 1 cup uncooked white rice
- 1 large onion, finely chopped
- 2 tbsp olive oil
- 1/4 cup pine nuts (optional)
- 1/4 cup fresh parsley, chopped
- 1/4 cup fresh mint, chopped
- 1/4 cup fresh dill, chopped
- Juice of 1 lemon
- Salt and pepper to taste
- 1 1/2 cups vegetable or chicken broth

Procedure

- In a skillet, heat olive oil over medium heat. Sauté onions until soft and translucent.
- Add rice, stirring to coat it with the oil. Cook for 5 minutes.
- Mix in pine nuts, parsley, mint, dill, salt, and pepper. Remove from heat.
- Lay out a grape leaf on a flat surface and place a small spoonful of the rice mixture in the center. Fold the sides over and roll tightly.
- Place the stuffed leaves seam-side down in a pot. Pour lemon juice and broth over them.
- Cover and simmer for 40 minutes until rice is tender. Serve warm or cold.

Nutritional Values (per serving)

- Calories: 120

- Protein: 3g
- Carbohydrates: 15g
- Fat: 5g
- Fiber: 2g

Health Benefits

- Grape leaves are rich in antioxidants, and the herbs used provide anti-inflammatory benefits. This dish is heart-healthy, low in calories, and supports digestion.

Greek-Style Yogurt Dip with Fresh Veggies

Preparation Time: 15 minutes

Cooking Time: None

Servings: 4-6

Ingredients

- 1 cup Greek yogurt
- 1 garlic clove, minced
- 1 tbsp olive oil
- 1 tbsp lemon juice
- 1 tbsp fresh dill, chopped
- 1 tbsp fresh parsley, chopped
- Salt and pepper to taste
- Assorted fresh veggies (cucumbers, bell peppers, carrots) for dipping

Procedure

- In a bowl, mix Greek yogurt, garlic, olive oil, lemon juice, dill, and parsley.
- Season with salt and pepper, adjusting to taste.
- Serve with fresh veggies arranged around the dip.

Nutritional Values (per serving)

- Calories: 80
- Protein: 6g
- Carbohydrates: 4g
- Fat: 4g
- Fiber: 1g

Health Benefits

- Greek yogurt is high in protein and probiotics, which are beneficial for gut health. The veggies add fiber and essential vitamins, making this dip both nutritious and satisfying.

Roasted Chickpeas with Sea Salt and Paprika

Preparation Time: 10 minutes

Cooking Time: 30 minutes

Servings: 4

Ingredients

- 1 can (15 oz) chickpeas, drained and rinsed
- 1 tbsp olive oil
- 1 tsp sea salt
- 1 tsp paprika
- 1/2 tsp garlic powder (optional)

Procedure

- Preheat the oven to 400°F (200°C).
- Pat chickpeas dry with a paper towel. Spread them on a baking sheet.
- Drizzle with olive oil, sprinkle with sea salt, paprika, and garlic powder. Toss to coat.
- Roast in the oven for 30 minutes, shaking the pan halfway through, until crispy.
- Allow to cool slightly before serving.

Nutritional Values (per serving)

- Calories: 120
- Protein: 5g
- Carbohydrates: 18g
- Fat: 3g
- Fiber: 4g

Health Benefits

- Chickpeas are an excellent source of plant-based protein, fiber, and iron. This snack is heart-healthy, promotes satiety, and supports digestion.

Mini Caprese Skewers with Basil and Balsamic Glaze

Preparation Time: 10 minutes

Cooking Time: 5 minutes

Servings: 4-6

Ingredients

- 1 pint cherry tomatoes
- 1 cup fresh mozzarella balls
- Fresh basil leaves
- 2 tbsp balsamic vinegar
- 1 tsp honey
- Toothpicks or small skewers

Procedure

- Thread cherry tomatoes, mozzarella balls, and basil leaves onto each skewer.
- In a small saucepan, heat balsamic vinegar and honey over low heat until it reduces to a glaze.
- Drizzle glaze over skewers before serving.

Nutritional Values (per skewer)

- Calories: 50
- Protein: 2g
- Carbohydrates: 3g
- Fat: 3g
- Fiber: 0.5g

Health Benefits

- This appetizer is a great source of calcium, antioxidants, and healthy fats. Tomatoes offer vitamin C and lycopene, while basil provides anti-inflammatory properties.

Roasted Olive Tapenade on Whole Grain Crackers

Preparation Time: 15 minutes

Cooking Time: 10 minutes

Servings: 4-6

Ingredients

- 1 cup mixed olives, pitted
- 1 tbsp capers
- 1 garlic clove
- 1 tbsp fresh lemon juice
- 2 tbsp olive oil
- Fresh ground pepper to taste
- Whole grain crackers

Procedure

- Preheat oven to 350°F (175°C).
- Combine olives, capers, garlic, lemon juice, and olive oil in a food processor. Pulse until chunky.
- Spread the tapenade on whole-grain crackers and arrange on a baking sheet.
- Roast in the oven for 10 minutes, just until warm.
- Serve warm or at room temperature.

Nutritional Values (per serving)

- Calories: 120
- Protein: 2g
- Carbohydrates: 6g
- Fat: 10g
- Fiber: 1g

Health Benefits

- Olives are rich in heart-healthy monounsaturated fats and antioxidants. This appetizer supports heart health, provides energy, and is a fiber-rich option for digestive health.

5

NOURISHING DESSERTS AND SWEET TREATS

Olive Oil and Lemon Cake

Preparation Time: 15 minutes

Cooking Time: 35-40 minutes

Servings: 8-10 slices

Ingredients:

- 1 1/2 cups all-purpose flour
- 1 cup sugar
- 1/2 teaspoon salt
- 1 teaspoon baking powder
- Zest of 2 lemons
- 3/4 cup extra-virgin olive oil
- 3 large eggs
- 1/4 cup fresh lemon juice
- 1/2 cup Greek yogurt
- Powdered sugar for dusting (optional)

Procedure:

- Preheat oven to 350°F (175°C). Grease and flour a round 9-inch cake pan.
- In a large bowl, combine the flour, sugar, salt, and baking powder.
- In a separate bowl, whisk together the lemon zest, olive oil, eggs, lemon juice, and Greek yogurt until smooth.
- Gradually fold the dry ingredients into the wet mixture, stirring until just combined.
- Pour the batter into the prepared cake pan and smooth the top.
- Bake for 35-40 minutes, or until a toothpick inserted into the center comes out clean.
- Let the cake cool completely before dusting with powdered sugar, if desired.

Nutritional Values (per slice):

- Calories: 220
- Protein: 3g
- Carbohydrates: 25g
- Fat: 12g
- Fiber: 1g

Health Benefits:

- This cake offers a source of heart-healthy fats from olive oil, which helps reduce inflammation. Lemon provides a dose of Vitamin C, which boosts immunity, while the yogurt contributes calcium and probiotics for gut health.

Honey-Drizzled Greek Yogurt with Walnuts

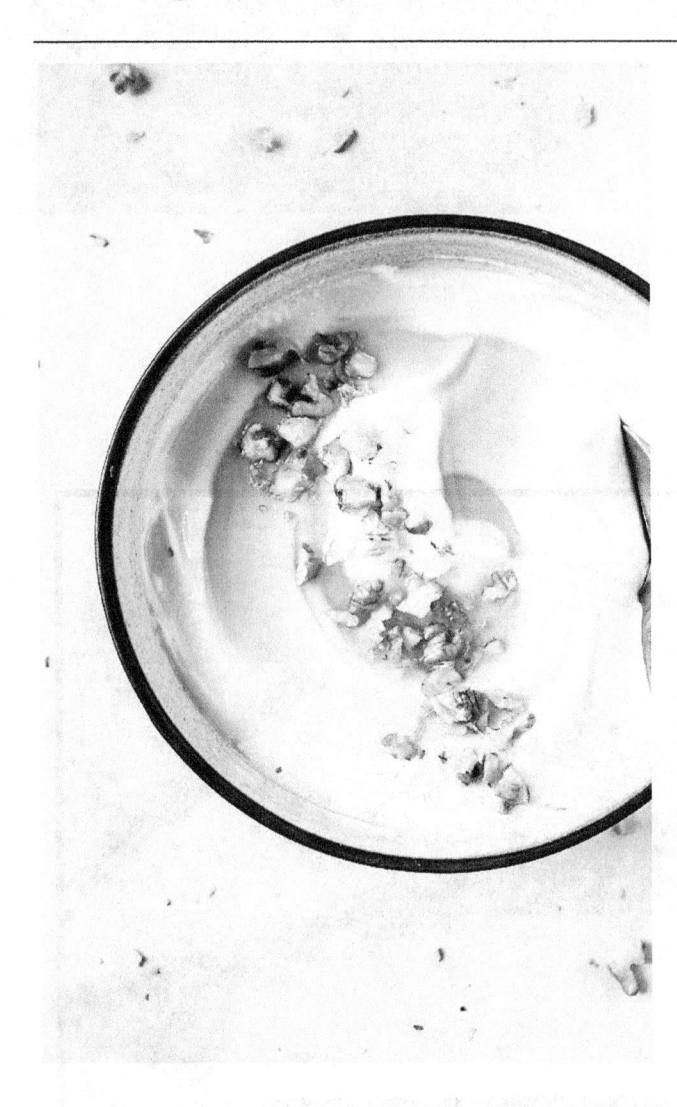

Preparation Time: 5 minutes

Cooking Time: None

Servings: 1 bowl

Ingredients:

- 1 cup plain Greek yogurt
- 1 tablespoon honey
- 2 tablespoons chopped walnuts
- 1/2 teaspoon cinnamon (optional)

Procedure:

- Spoon the Greek yogurt into a serving bowl.
- Drizzle the honey over the yogurt.
- Sprinkle with walnuts and a dash of cinnamon if desired.
- Serve immediately and enjoy.

Nutritional Values (per bowl):

- Calories: 200
- Protein: 10g
- Carbohydrates: 18g
- Fat: 10g
- Fiber: 1g

Health Benefits:

- Greek yogurt provides protein and probiotics, which support muscle maintenance and gut health. Walnuts are rich in omega-3 fatty acids, promoting brain health, while honey adds natural sweetness along with antioxidants.

Poached Pears with Cinnamon and Clove

Preparation Time: 10 minutes

Cooking Time: 20-25 minutes

Servings: 4

Ingredients:

- 4 ripe pears, peeled and cored
- 3 cups water
- 1/2 cup honey or sugar
- 1 cinnamon stick
- 3 whole cloves
- Juice of 1 lemon

Procedure:

- In a large saucepan, combine water, honey or sugar, cinnamon stick, cloves, and lemon juice. Bring to a simmer.
- Add the pears to the saucepan and simmer for 20-25 minutes or until tender, turning occasionally.
- Remove the pears from the poaching liquid and let them cool slightly.
- Serve warm or chilled, with a drizzle of the poaching liquid if desired.

Nutritional Values (per pear):

- Calories: 150
- Protein: 1g
- Carbohydrates: 35g
- Fat: 0g
- Fiber: 5g

Health Benefits:

- Pears are high in dietary fiber, which aids digestion and helps control blood sugar. Cinnamon and clove add antioxidants and have anti-inflammatory properties, enhancing this simple dessert's health value.

Fresh Fig and Almond Tart

Preparation Time: 20 minutes

Cooking Time: 25-30 minutes

Servings: 8 slices

Ingredients:

- 1 sheet puff pastry
- 1 cup almond flour
- 1/4 cup sugar
- 1/4 cup butter, softened
- 1 egg
- 1 teaspoon vanilla extract
- 8-10 fresh figs, sliced

Procedure:

- Preheat oven to 375°F (190°C). Place the puff pastry on a baking sheet and score a border around the edges.
- In a bowl, mix the almond flour, sugar, butter, egg, and vanilla until smooth.
- Spread the almond mixture over the puff pastry, leaving the border clean.
- Arrange the fig slices on top of the almond filling.
- Bake for 25-30 minutes, until the pastry is golden and the figs are tender.
- Let cool before slicing.

Nutritional Values (per slice):

- Calories: 230
- Protein: 5g
- Carbohydrates: 22g
- Fat: 14g
- Fiber: 2g

Health Benefits:

- Figs provide fiber, antioxidants, and vitamins, supporting digestion and heart health. Almonds are rich in healthy fats and vitamin E, promoting skin health and reducing inflammation.

Dark Chocolate and Nut Clusters

Preparation Time: 10 minutes

Cooking Time: 10 minutes (plus cooling)

Servings: 12 clusters

Ingredients:

- 1 cup dark chocolate chips (70% cocoa or higher)
- 1/2 cup almonds, roughly chopped
- 1/2 cup walnuts, roughly chopped
- 1/4 cup dried cranberries or cherries (optional)

Procedure:

- Melt the dark chocolate in a double boiler or microwave in short intervals.
- Stir in the chopped nuts and dried fruit (if using).
- Spoon small clusters onto a parchment-lined baking sheet.
- Let the clusters cool and harden before serving.

Nutritional Values (per cluster):

- Calories: 100
- Protein: 2g
- Carbohydrates: 8g
- Fat: 7g
- Fiber: 2g

Health Benefits:

- Dark chocolate is high in antioxidants, promoting heart health and improving mood. Nuts provide omega-3 fats and protein, supporting brain and heart health, while dried cranberries add a touch of natural sweetness and antioxidants.

SHOPPING LIST

Produce	1 bunch fresh basil
Fruits	1 bunch fresh cilantro
4 lemons	1 bag arugula or mixed greens
4 oranges	Proteins
8 pears	1 dozen large eggs
8-10 fresh figs	1 lb chicken breast
4 apples	1 lb salmon fillets
2 bananas	1 lb shrimp, peeled and deveined
1 pineapple	1 lb ground turkey or chicken
1 pint strawberries	1 package of firm tofu
1 pint blueberries	1 lb beef or lamb (optional for variety)
1 bunch grapes	1 lb white fish fillets (such as cod or tilapia)
1 melon (cantaloupe or honeydew)	Dairy
1 bunch fresh mint	1 container Greek yogurt (plain, 32 oz)
Vegetables	1 pint milk or plant-based milk (such as almond or oat milk)
1 head garlic	8 oz feta cheese
2 large onions	8 oz goat cheese
3 bell peppers (any color)	1 block Parmesan cheese
1 cucumber	1 pint heavy cream or plant-based cream alternative
1 bag baby spinach	1 pack sliced mozzarella
1 bunch kale	Grains & Breads
2 large tomatoes	1 loaf whole-grain or sourdough bread
1 zucchini	
1 bunch fresh parsley	

1 package whole-grain pita or flatbreads
1 package whole-grain pasta
1 bag brown rice or quinoa
1 package whole-grain couscous
1 pack whole-wheat tortillas or wraps
1 bag oats
Nuts, Seeds, & Snacks
1 bag almonds
1 bag walnuts
1 bag chia seeds
1 bag sunflower seeds
1 bag pumpkin seeds
1 package dried cranberries or cherries
Canned Goods
1 can chickpeas
1 can black beans
1 can cannellini beans
1 can whole peeled tomatoes
1 can coconut milk
Oils, Vinegars, & Condiments
Extra-virgin olive oil (16 oz bottle)
Coconut oil (optional for baking)
Balsamic vinegar
Red wine vinegar
Apple cider vinegar
Tahini (for sauces and dressings)
Dijon mustard

Honey
Maple syrup
Dark chocolate (70% or higher)
Herbs & Spices
Sea salt
Black pepper
Cinnamon sticks
Ground cinnamon
Ground cumin
Ground paprika
Ground coriander
Ground turmeric
Dried oregano
Dried basil
Dried thyme
Cloves (whole or ground)
Chili flakes (optional)
Baking Essentials
All-purpose flour (or gluten-free flour)
Almond flour
Baking powder
Baking soda
Sugar
Powdered sugar
Brown sugar

CONCLUSION

As we reach the end of this Mediterranean Diet Cookbook for Seniors, let's take a moment to reflect on the journey we've embarked on together. From vibrant salads and nourishing mains to delightful, guilt-free desserts, each recipe in this book has been thoughtfully crafted to bring the best of Mediterranean living to your kitchen. These recipes aren't just about feeding your body—they're designed to nourish your soul, support your health, and keep you feeling your best.

Living in your golden years should be about more than just maintaining health; it should be about thriving with energy, joy, and flavor. The Mediterranean diet embodies a lifestyle that prioritizes simplicity, balance, and pleasure, offering a sustainable way to eat that never feels like a chore. The meals are abundant in nutrient-rich ingredients like leafy greens, whole grains, lean proteins, and healthy fats, which collectively support heart health, brain function, and longevity.

Incorporating these recipes into your daily life brings so many benefits beyond the plate. You'll enjoy the pleasures of cooking and eating, discover new tastes and textures, and connect with a tradition known for its powerful health benefits. Even more importantly, this diet can help you maintain a vibrant quality of life by lowering inflammation, supporting mobility, and boosting mood.

As you continue with these recipes, remember that each meal is an opportunity to care for yourself in a meaningful way. Take your time as you cook, savor the process, and share these dishes with loved ones whenever you can. The Mediterranean diet is a celebration of life's simple pleasures, enjoyed one meal at a time.

Thank you for letting this book be a part of your wellness journey. May it inspire you to embrace a life full of good food, cherished moments, and better health. Here's to a future filled with delicious dishes, vibrant health, and the joy of knowing you're giving your body the care it deserves. Let's make every meal count, savoring the journey to lasting well-being and enjoying each bite along the way.

Made in the USA
Columbia, SC
03 June 2025